SUCCESS
STARTS WITH
ATTITUDE

50 Ways to Refuel, Recharge and Reenergize
Yourself in Business and Life

JAMES MAL

Contributing Author to and Associa
book series *Chicken Sou*

Published by James Malinchak International, Inc.

Copyright © 2001 James Malinchak International, Inc.
Second Printing – 2006

Printed in the United States of America

Library of Congress Control Number: 2005936048

Malinchak, James
      Success Starts With Attitude / by James Malinchak
      Library of Congress Cataloging-in-Publication Data
      ISBN: 0-9646924-3-0

Warning – Disclaimer
The purpose of this book is to educate and entertain. The author or publisher does not guarantee that anyone following the techniques, suggestions, tips, ideas, or strategies will become successful. The author and publisher shall have neither liability or responsibility to anyone with respect to any loss or damage caused, or alleged to be caused, directly or indirectly by the information contained in this book.

About James Malinchak

James Malinchak has delivered over 2,200 motivational presentations at conferences and meetings worldwide, and was named **Consummate Speaker** of the Year by Sharing Ideas professional speakers' magazine. He has appeared in *USA Today*, *The Wall Street Journal* and several hundred other publications.

James began his sales career right out of college as a stockbroker with a major Wall Street Investment Firm and was awarded **Most Outstanding Performance (twice)** and **#1 in New Account Openings (twice)**. While in his twenties, James became a partner in a company that handled the investments for many famous entertainers, authors and professional athletes.

Currently, James owns three businesses, has authored eight books, and has read and researched over 1,500 books on personal and professional development. He is a **Contributing Author** to, and serves as **Associate Editor** for, the **#1 New York Times Best-Selling** book series *Chicken Soup for the Soul,*® with his own personal stories published in *Chicken Soup for the Teenage Soul, Chicken Soup for the Kid's Soul* and *Chicken Soup for the Prisoner's Soul.* James is the **Co-Author** of the upcoming book, *Chicken Soup for the Athlete's Soul.*

For more resources and to subscribe to James' **FREE "Success Tips" ezine newsletter,** visit **www.Malinchak.com**

Refuel, Recharge and Reenergize Yourself!

What happens when the vehicle you are driving gets low on fuel or the battery in your cell phone gets low on energy? The vehicle and cell phone will not operate at their fullest capacity. The same is true for us as individuals.

We all have times in our lives when our personal fuel tanks get low on fuel or our internal batteries get low on energy. If we don't continue to refuel, recharge and reenergize ourselves we can't perform at our fullest potential. We lack focus, motivation and enthusiasm, while our results become mediocre.

This book offers simple suggestions that will help you to refuel, recharge and reenergize so you produce greater results in business and life!

-James Malinchak

1.
Success Starts With Attitude

Why does attitude play such an important role in our success? In my constant and never-ending search to understand what elevates human potential, one answer consistently prevails:

Attitude = Beliefs = Actions = Results

Success begins with our internal state of mind. What we focus on through the attitudes we choose to maintain is who we become and what we achieve, both positively and negatively.

"Be careful what you think about because you will surely get it."
-Thomas Carlisle

2.
Attitude = Results

You have the ability within to manifest an incredible power that can lead you toward creating and maintaining greater personal and professional results. Whether you're dealing with customers, clients, employers, employees, family members, personal relationships or personal issues, your results will be determined by the attitude you choose to bring to each situation. If you don't like the results you're getting, change your attitude.

"The minute you begin to change your attitude is the minute YOU CAN begin to change your results."

-James Malinchak

3.
Which Attitude Station
Are You Tuning Into?

If you tune into the wrong station, don't expect to get the right music. But the great thing about attitude is that it doesn't require a big change. If you have a little static on the station you're listening to, simply adjust the dial and you can get rid of the static and tune into the station that plays the sweet sounding music that you want to hear.

**"The greatest discovery of my generation
is that human beings can alter their lives
by altering their attitudes."**

-William James

4.
Get a Strong Desire

Given the choice between two individuals; a person with a high I.Q., but a weak desire to succeed or a person with an average I.Q., but a strong desire to succeed I'll choose the second individual every time.

REMEMBER:

"It's not how much smarts you have, it's how much HEART you have!"

-James Malinchak

5.
Be Thankful for Adversity

As you pursue dreams and goals, accept the fact that you will face adversity. Be thankful for the adversity. It can make you wiser, stronger and better. Past failures, disappointments and rejection can only be used in two ways: To pull yourself up or to pull yourself down. Which way *you allow yourself* to be pulled is your choice.

REMEMBER:

**"Adversity is the best university
because adversity will teach you lessons
if you will only allow your eyes and ears
to catch the message."**

-James Malinchak

6.

The Next Time You Want to Quit, Get Inspired By These People

Danielle "Rudy" Ruettiger was turned down for nine years before getting his life story made into a major motion movie called *Rudy*.

Jack Canfield and Mark Victor Hansen created the #1 best-selling book series, *Chicken Soup for the Soul*® after initially being rejected by 33 publishers and receiving a total of 144 rejections.

Thomas Edison invented the light bulb after 14,000 unsuccessful attempts.

At age nine, Wilma Rudolph contracted scarlet fever, was forced to wear a metal leg brace and was told she would never walk correctly. Wilma Rudolph went on to win three Olympic Gold Medals in track and field and was proclaimed one of America's fastest runners.

Running a four-minute mile was inconceivable until it was accomplished by Roger Bannister. Today, many people can do it.

"Whether you think you can or think you can't, you are right."

-Henry Ford

7.
Eliminate the FEAR

Remember what fear stands for:
False **E**vidence **A**ppearing **R**eal

Psychologists tell us that human beings are born with only two fears; the fear of falling and the fear of loud noises. All other fears are self-imposed, which means they can be overcome.

How do you overcome fear? By taking action and busting through the *perceived* fear. Fear is perceived because any fear you have other than the two mentioned above were created by you. Have the courage to act in spite of your *perceived* fears.

"All our dreams can come true –
if we have the courage to pursue them."

-Walt Disney

8.
Never Give Up

Difficult times are only tests that life gives us to see if we really want to achieve our dreams. Once proven that you do have the desire by not giving up, the difficult times seem to disappear.

REMEMBER:

"Tough times are just like storms, eventually they pass. So you have to ride out the storm."
-James Malinchak

"Tough times don't last, tough people do."
-Dr. Robert Schuller

9.
Nothing is Impossible

Achieving dreams and goals may be difficult, but I don't believe they're impossible to achieve. As human beings, we have the ability to achieve anything we desire. If you're not achieving what you desire then it's simply because of a choice you made to stop pursuing the dream or goal.

"Take the 'T' out of can't."
-James Malinchak

"When you see the word impossible you should always see *I'm possible.*"
-James Malinchak

10.
You Only Fail If You Quit!

Consider Abraham Lincoln:

1831 – Failed in business
1832 – Lost election for Legislature
1833 – Failed in business a second time
1836 – Had a nervous breakdown
1838 – Lost election for Speaker
1840 – Lost election for Elector
1843 – Lost election for Congress
1848 – Lost election for Congress
1855 – Lost election for Senate
1856 – Lost election for Vice President
1858 – Lost election for Senate
1860 – Elected President of the United States

"Every adversity, every failure, every heartache carries with it the seed of an equal or greater benefit."

–Napoleon Hill

11.
Take Responsibility

Too many people blame others if they fail to achieve a goal. They make statements such as:

"If only I had better training…"
"If only I had a manager who motivated me more…"

You are responsible for your own happiness or sadness, success or failure, prosperity or poverty.

REMEMBER:

"Others may help you to develop your ability, but you're the only one who can use it."

-James Malinchak

12.
Get Inspired By Others

I have a very good friend named Joe Martin who lives in Tallahassee, Florida. Joe and I first met a few years ago when we were speaking at the same conference. When I first met Joe, there was something that I immediately liked about him. However, I couldn't quite figure out what it was.

As we finished our talks I invited him to dinner. I thought we would only spend an hour eating and talking. But the more Joe talked, the more I wanted to listen and learn more about him. I am always intrigued by stories of people who have overcome tremendous obstacles in order to create a successful life. What Joe had to overcome amazed me.

Joe grew up in Liberty City in Miami, FL which is one of the worst inner city ghettos in the United States. He said, "James, you wouldn't believe some of the things I had seen growing up as a teenager. Drugs, prostitution and people killing people."

Joe said that one time he called his mother on the telephone but he couldn't hear her because of loud noise in the background, which he thought was coming from the television. So he asked his mother if she would kindly turn the volume down. She responded by saying that she didn't have the television on. With amazement Joe asked, "Well, what's all that noise in the background?" Shockingly, Joe's mother responded, "Oh, people are just out back shooting at each other!"

Joe said that when he heard this he immediately knew he had to do something to help get his mother, his sister and himself out of that ghetto or he knew they could be killed. So he changed his attitude and decided to make a commitment to better educate himself. Joe said, "It wasn't a big change, I just changed my attitude and looked at myself and my future differently." When Joe did that he found out that his grades in school improved. They improved enough to get him through high school and into college.

While in college, Joe continued to keep his attitude tuned into the right station and as a result his grades and overall success improved tremendously. As a matter of fact, he went on to graduate college with a 3.8 grade point average (GPA) and was named the top student in his class. Then, Joe went on to become the youngest person in the history of the state of Florida to ever become a college professor. He accomplished it by age 24. Currently, Joe's a professor at the University of West Florida in Pensacola, FL where he inspires students to overcome challenges and pursue their purpose.

> ## "It doesn't matter where you start. It matters where you finish."
> ### *-Joe Martin*

> ## "Sometimes the best fighting position is on your knees; we call it prayer – the ultimate in hand to hand combat."
> ### *-Joe Martin*

13.
It's Not the Circumstances, It's How YOU React

You will be successful the minute
YOU decide to be successful…period!
Blaming others or certain circumstances
for any failures you experience is foolish.
You may not be able to control certain
circumstances, but YOU CAN control how
you react to the circumstances. And how
you react to the circumstances will
determine the end result.

**"Things turn out best for those who
make the best of the way things turn out."**
-John Wooden

14.
Continue to Learn

I'm sure you heard the phrase, "Knowledge is power!" How true it is. The more you learn, the stronger you grow. Also, the more you grow, the more diverse your background becomes. The more diverse your background becomes, the more interesting and influential you will be to others.

Open your mind to new ideas and opinions by reading books, attending workshops and meeting new people. Make a consistent effort to continue your own personal learning process.

"Anyone who stops learning is old – whether at twenty or eighty. Anyone who keeps learning stays young. The greatest thing in life is to keep your mind young."

-Henry Ford

15.
Read 30-Minutes a Day

Read a self-improvement book 30-minutes each day.
I recommend the first 15-minutes when you awake in
the morning and 15-minutes before going to bed at
night. Start your day and end your evening with
positive, uplifting information that plants
success seeds in your mental garden.

**"You are what you are and where you are
because of what's gone into your mind. You
an change what you are and where you are
by changing what goes into your mind."**

-Zig Ziglar

16.
Read Books, Listen to Audio Programs and Attend Seminars

It amazes me how many people complain about not reaching higher levels, making more money and increasing their business. Yet, they aren't willing to invest a small amount of money in self-help books, audio programs and seminars that can immediately provide ideas, strategies and shortcuts for reaching their goals. One reason many fail to invest in themselves is because of ego. I often hear, *"I don't need to buy those motivational books and audio programs or attend seminars because I've been in my industry for 'x' number of years and I'm an experienced professional!"*

"It's what you learn after you know it all that counts."
-John Wooden

17.
Never Stop Dreaming

Nothing great has ever been achieved without first dreaming about it. Dreaming allows us to picture what we most desire. To achieve a dream, you must first form a mental image of how you would feel and what positive results you would experience when your dream is realized. Anything you wish to accomplish in life must first be pictured in your mind, felt in your heart and desired in your soul.

"Champions aren't made in the gyms. Champions are made from something they have deep inside them – a desire, a dream, a vision."

-Muhammad Ali

18.
Don't Be Afraid to Fail

There's a chance you may fail while trying to achieve your goals. You must understand and accept this. No one said success would be easy. The important thing is to never quit or give-up when you fail. Successful people aren't afraid to fail because they understand that failure is a part of trying. I would rather fail trying to achieve a goal than to not even try at all. Don't quit when faced with failure. You may be closer to your goal than you think.

"Success seems to be largely a matter of hanging on after others have let go."

-William Feather

"In the middle of difficulty lies opportunity."

-Albert Einstein

19.
Focus On Your Strengths

Many people spend too much time focusing on their weaknesses rather than their strengths.
Therefore, they minimize their potential by creating incorrect images of themselves.

Evaluate yourself to determine if you are focusing more on your strengths or weaknesses. Discover what you're really good at and determine how you can use those strengths to your advantage.

"Don't let what you cannot do interfere with what you can do."
-John Wooden

20.
Associate With Winners

The type of people you associate with reflects the type of person you will become. If you associate with negative people, then you will eventually become a negative person. If you associate with positive people who have dreams and goals, then you will develop successful, winning habits.

"There is little difference in people, but that little difference makes a big difference. The little difference is attitude. The big difference is whether it is positive or negative."

-W. Clement Stone

21.
Watch Out for Negative People

As you begin pursuing certain goals, you may encounter people who will criticize and try to convince you that achieving certain goals in your life aren't possible. Stay away from these negative thinking people. Those who tell you that it can't be done are simply jealous or haven't really achieved their goals. Don't worry about what others think about your ability to achieve a goal. It only matters what you think and believe about yourself.

"As he thinketh in his heart, so is he."
-Proverbs 23:7

22.
Appreciate Your Loved Ones

<u>Thank You Family</u>™...*by James Malinchak*

For teaching me wrong from right
And for encouraging me to keep my dreams in sight

For showing me not to let obstacles keep me down
And for creating a smile from my frown

For saying that you care about me
And for showing just how special love should be

For wiping my tears away when I'm feeling sad
And for calming me down when I tend to get mad

For helping others with the good that you do
And for teaching me that I should help others, too

For hugging me when I am feeling blue
And whispering into my ear I love you

Thank you, family, for all that you do
I don't know where I would be if it weren't for you

Thank You Family. Copyright © 1998 by James Malinchak.

23.
Enjoy Success, But Always Keep Your Family Your Top Priority

A Brother's Voice™

by James Malinchak

Most people have an inspiration in their life. Maybe it's a talk with someone you respect or an experience. Whatever the inspiration, it tends to make you look at life from a different perspective. My inspiration came from my sister Vicki, a kind and caring person. She didn't care about accolades or being written about in newspapers. All she wanted was to share her love with the people she cared about, her family and friends.

The summer before my junior year of college, I received a phone call from my father saying that Vicki was rushed to the hospital. She had collapsed and the right side of her body was paralyzed. The preliminary indications were that she suffered a stroke. However, test results confirmed it was much more serious. There was a malignant brain tumor causing her paralysis. Her doctors didn't give her more than three months to live.

I remember wondering how this could happen? The day before Vicki was perfectly fine. Now, her life was coming to an end at such a young age.

After overcoming the initial shock and feeling of emptiness, I decided that Vicki needed hope and encouragement. She needed someone to make her believe that she would overcome this obstacle. I became Vicki's coach. Everyday we would visualize the tumor shrinking and everything that we talked about was positive. I even posted a sign on her hospital room door that read, "If you have any negative thoughts, leave them at the door." I was determined to help Vicki beat the tumor. She and I made a deal that we called 50-50. I would do 50% of the fighting and Vicki would do the other 50%.

The month of August arrived and it was time to begin my junior year of college 3,000 miles away. I was unsure whether I should leave or stay with Vicki. I made the mistake of telling her that I might not leave for school. She became angry and said not to worry because she would be fine. There was Vicki lying ill in a hospital bed telling me not to worry. I realized that if I stayed it might send a message that she was dying and I didn't want her believing that. Vicki needed to believe that she could win against the tumor.

Leaving that night feeling it might be the last time I would ever see Vicki alive was the most difficult thing I have ever done. While at school, I never stopped fighting my 50% for her. Every night before falling asleep I would talk to Vicki, hoping that there was some way she could hear me. I would say, "Vicki, I'm fighting for you and I will never quit. As long as you never quit fighting, we will beat this."

A few months had passed and she was still holding on. I was talking with an elderly friend and she asked about Vicki's situation. I told her that she was getting worse but that she wasn't quitting. My friend asked a question that really made me think. She said, "Do you think the reason she hasn't let go is because she doesn't want to let you down?" Maybe she was right? Maybe I was selfish for encouraging Vicki to keep fighting? That night before falling asleep, I said to her, "Vicki, I understand that you're in a lot of pain and that you might like to let go. If you do, then I want you to. We didn't lose because you never quit fighting. If you want to go on to a better place then I understand. We will be together again. I love you and I'll always be with you wherever you are."

Early the next morning, my mother called to tell me that Vicki had passed away.

"We never appreciate the value of water until the well runs dry."

-Benjamin Franklin

I've never heard of anyone close to death saying, *I wish I would have spent more time working*. It's always, *I wish I would have spent more time with the people I love and care about."*

-Unknown

24.
Be a Good Person

- Remember what's important in life: God, good health, safety, peace, happiness and the people you love and care about.

- Always be honest, loyal and love your significant other.

- Show support by always being there for family and friends.

- Listen when your family and friends need to talk.

- Show respect, loyalty and love by always being honest and true to your word.

- Don't argue or cause resentment. Life is too short!

- Thank those who have helped you.

- Go out of your way to help others.

- Make people smile and laugh.

- Encourage and help children and elderly people. They need it more than anyone.

- Treat others as you would like to be treated.

- Don't screw people over.

- Keep your promise and your word.

- Take responsibility for yourself and your actions.

- Give respect to get respect.

- Apologize with sincerity if you are wrong.

- Tell those you really love and care about that they are important to you. Then tell them again!

"You have to look in the mirror when you awake in the morning and before you go to bed at night. And the mirror doesn't lie about what it sees."

-Unknown

25.
YOU Choose Your Happiness

Too many people have the misconception that their happiness is determined by other people. Happiness is simply a state of mind. Your life will become more enjoyable the minute YOU CHOOSE to be happy. Don't look for happiness from others or external factors because happiness comes from within.

"Why should my happiness depend on the thoughts of what's going on in someone else's head?"

-Ralph Waldo Emerson

26.

Be Willing to Serve Others By Putting Other Peoples Need's Before Your Own

You Never Know Who's Listening™

by James Malinchak

A friend of mine named Cynthia asked me if I would be interested in talking to a group of teenagers about the skills necessary for succeeding in the real world. I love helping teenagers achieve success, so naturally, I accepted.

As we were driving to the talk, Cynthia said that there was something that she didn't tell me about this group of teenagers. My first thought was that there would be hundreds of them, and she was worried that I may be a little nervous, but that wasn't it, at all.

Cynthia was taking me to speak to teenagers in prison. That's right, prison! She began preparing me for what I was about to face. She said that I would be speaking to some of the most dangerous, messed-up kids in Southern California. Some were in for theft, arson, battery, and even murder. She said that I could tell who the murderers were, because they would be dressed in orange work clothes.

Cynthia was also kind enough to mention that these teenagers were only permitted one hour of recreation per week, and that I would be "stealing" their hour of free time. Didn't this just make me feel wonderful?

As the inmates came into the room, you could see that they really didn't want to be there, but I went there to do a job, and I wasn't going to be discouraged. Midway through my talk, some began heckling me while others simply weren't paying attention. I thought to myself, *What a waste of time.*

My talk was only twenty minutes, so they had forty minutes of free time to do what they wanted. Thank God! The only problem was that I wasn't permitted to leave until their full hour was up. So Cynthia and I remained in the room with the prisoners anxiously watching the clock.

All of a sudden I noticed that one of the biggest, baddest-looking teenagers I have ever seen in my life was walking toward us. He was dressed in orange, about six-feet-five, weighing around 225. I became more and more nervous the closer he got.

Finally, he was no more than two feet away, and I thought to myself, *This guy is going to take a swing at me.* To my surprise he extended his hand and said, "Your talk was great. At first, I wasn't really paying attention because I was thinking of killing a prisoner named Joe tonight. But when you said, 'Wouldn't this world be a better place if we all just simply loved and cared for each other?' – it really hit me. All of a sudden, I began feeling love toward Joe, and I feel like I can do something with my life.

I just wanted to say thank you, and I want you to know that I listened and appreciate that you came here tonight. No one cares about us. It means a lot to me that you took the time to come here. Do you think you could come back again?"

It was difficult for me to speak as I was choked with emotion. At that moment, I realized that I had done the right thing by speaking to the inmates. I was able to help at least one person, and that's all that mattered.

I reached out and hugged him with one of the tightest grips I've ever applied. As we hugged, I whispered to him, "God Bless You!"

Surprisingly, he replied, "No sir, God Bless You for coming here. You saved two lives tonight – Joe's and mine!"

You Never Know Who's Listening. Copyright © 1999 by James Malinchak.

"What you remember, what you measure yourself by, what you cling to as you get older is what you have done as a family, what you have done for others, your own naked humanity."

-Former First Lady Barbara Bush

27.
Be a Goal Setter

The purpose of goals is to focus your attention. You will not progress toward achievement until you clearly define and set goals. Not setting goals can be compared to trying to drive a car to a place you've never visited. How can you expect to reach your destination without proper direction? The same is true of anything you are striving to achieve. You need to set goals – your road map.

"If you don't know where you are going, how can you expect to get there?"

-Basil S. Walsh

28.
James Malinchak's
7 Steps for Achieving Any Goal

1. **Get a specific GOAL**
   Ask Yourself: "What do I want?"

2. **Develop a PURPOSE for the goal**
   Ask Yourself: "Why do I want it?" (This ignites your PASSION)

3. **List OTHERS who can help you achieve your goal**
   Ask Yourself: "Who I can learn from who has already achieved this goal? Who do I know who has contacts that could help me?"

4. **Create your PLAN**
   Ask Yourself: "Which steps must I take to reach my goal?"

5. **Think of possible OBSTACLES and SOLUTIONS**
   Ask Yourself: "Which roadblocks may arise and how will I overcome them?"

6. **TAKE ACTION Now!**
   Ask Yourself: "Which steps will I immediately begin?"

7. **EVALUATE your progress and make necessary adjustments**
   Ask Yourself: "Am I on target with my current plan?"

www.Malinchak.com

29.
The Next Time You Want to Quit, Get Inspired By These People

Talk show host Oprah Winfrey grew up in a shack in Mississippi. She's now one of the most successful women in the world with an estimated net worth of over $900 million.

Ted Turner was told his plans for a 24-hour news network would never work. Today, CNN is watched globally.

Fred Smith was told by experts that his idea for an overnight delivery service was ridiculous. Today, Federal Express is used worldwide.

Michael Jordan was once cut from his high school basketball team.

Babe Ruth hit 714 home runs in his baseball career, but he also struck out 1,330 times.

Colonel Saunders was rejected 1,009 times before selling his recipe that led to the creation of Kentucky Fried Chicken, now KFC.

"Success is how high you bounce after you hit bottom."
-General George S. Patton

30.
Become a Master Networker

Contacts can serve as a tremendous shortcut to success. The more people you know, the more opportunities you will have. Get to know as many people as possible. I'm a firm believer that in today's society who you know can help get you ahead faster than anything else. Diversify your contacts by meeting people of different races, religions, political beliefs, ages or genders.

"Your career, business, income and net worth will not increase until your contacts increase."

-James Malinchak

31.
Stay in Touch With Contacts

Why is it important to stay in touch with your contacts? You never know who knows whom, where it could lead or which opportunities could arise for you. How do you stay in touch? Send thank you notes, congratulatory cards, thinking of you cards, birthday cards, holiday cards, anniversary cards and basic letters. Call certain contacts periodically and if you happen to be in their area, take them to lunch or at least give them a quick call to say hello. Today, with the power of the Internet, the easiest way to stay in touch is to accumulate email addresses in an e-address book and send emails.

"Meet people then stay in touch with them forever. You just never know where it could lead."

-James Malinchak

32.
The Only Business Philosophy
That Really Matters

I have a simple business philosophy:

Any business that doesn't continuously attract
new customers and consistently keep existing
customers will not be in business very long!

**"Do what you do so well and so uniquely
that your customers can't help but tell
others about you."**

-Disney principle

33.
Ask for Business Referrals

Most friends, customers and associates are happy to refer others to you or help you with an introduction to someone they know. But you have to ask. Why is it important to focus on building your business through referrals? Consider the following three reasons: (1) Receiving referrals is the easiest and fastest way to build a successful and lucrative business; (2) People would prefer to do business with you if you are referred to them by someone they trust; and (3) Most business professionals are forced out of business because they don't have a continuous stream of new customers/clients.

"If you don't ask then you won't get. But if you will simply ask for what you want, then you will be amazed at what you will get."

-James Malinchak

34.
Take GREAT Care of Customers

You aren't doing your customers a favor
by servicing them. They are doing you a
favor by allowing you to do so.

Why? Because they can choose to spend their
money on someone else's product or service
and they will if they feel you aren't taking
care of their needs.

**"Devote an hour a day to thinking about nothing
other than ways you might be of greater or
better service to your customers."**

-Earl Nightingale

35.
Focus on Customer Service

There is nothing more important to the success of your business than the happiness of your customers. Forget about implementing strategic plans, drafting business plans and creating fancy promotional materials. Without satisfied and loyal customers all those other aspects of running your business don't matter. If you doubt it, then try running your business without the customers. Too many businesses spend an enormous amount of time on various aspects of running a business rather than concentrating on <u>the</u> most important aspect; taking care of customers so they never want to leave you.

"Nothing beats customer satisfaction."

-Jim McCann
Founder, 1-800-Flowers

36.

The Next Time You Want to Quit, Get Inspired By These People

Mary Higgins Clark, who earns approximately $12 million for each suspense novel she writes, started as a flight attendant before pursuing her dream of writing books.

Heather Whitestone won the 1994 Miss America crown despite being 100% deaf in one ear and 95% deaf in her other.

Walt Disney was told he lacked creative talent after submitting his first drawings to a studio.

Ron Rice, founder of the mega-million dollar sun tanning oil and lotion company Hawaiian Tropic, began his idea as a mixture of a few ingredients in a garbage can in his garage.

Mary Kay Ash sold a total of $1.50 worth of products at her first beauty product show. Today, her company, Mary Kay Cosmetics, is a worldwide leader in beauty care.

At age 74, Benjamin Roll passed the bar exam to practice law after taking twelve years to get his degree and after failing 14 previous tries at passing the bar.

"All things are difficult before they are easy!"

-Thomas Fuller

37.
Work as a TEAM

Nobody ever achieves a dream
without the help of others.

Michael Jordan was one of the
highest-scoring basketball players in the NBA
when he first began playing for the Chicago Bulls.

But he didn't achieve his dream of winning
the NBA championship until other key players
were assembled and they began playing as a TEAM!

REMEMBER:

"It takes teamwork to make your dream work!"
-James Malinchak

38.
Lead to Succeed

To effectively lead others, remember the
7 Steps for Effective Leadership,™
which correspond to the letters in the word

LEADERS:

L: Continue to **LEARN**
E: Eliminate **EXCUSES**
A: Maintain a Positive **ATTITUDE**
D: Make **DECISIONS** for WE not me
E: **ENCOURAGE** Team Members
R: **REWARD** Team Members
S: **SERVE** Others

"Leadership is not a right – it's a responsibility."

-John Maxwell

39.
Make Others Feel Appreciated By Offering Praise

Mastering the art of praising others isn't time consuming and doesn't require immense planning. Simply say something uplifting and encouraging such as, "nice job," "I'm proud of you," "you're doing great," "I appreciate you going the extra mile," "thank you for working a little longer on the project," and "I really value having you as a part of my team." Also, get in the habit of leaving notes and cards offering similar messages.

"Great leaders encourage rather than discourage."

-James Malinchak

40.
Don't Just Talk When You Communicate With Others…Listen

One thing I consistently do is communicate with different people. One percent of what I learn is from talking with them. The other 99% is from listening to them!

"You can make more friends in two months by becoming interested in other people, than you can in two years by trying to get people interested in you."

-Dale Carnegie

41.

The Next Time You Want to Quit, Get Inspired By These People

A CNN executive personally pulled Katie Couric off the air and told her she had no future in television. She went on to become co-host of NBC's program *The Today Show* and earns an estimated $10 million a year salary.

J.K. Rowling only received a modest $5,000 advance for writing her first book. Publishing experts are predicting that she will earn an estimated $1 billion in future revenue from her *Harry Potter* series.

Prior to Sarian Bouma building a multimillion-dollar office cleaning company, she was a single mother on welfare.

Comedian/Actor Billy Crystal started out as a ticket taker at a movie theater.

Randy Travis was rejected by almost every record company in Nashville.

Jim Abbott pitched in the major leagues despite having only one hand.

Ray Charles was told by teachers that he couldn't play the piano.

Actor Harrison Ford started out as a carpenter.

"The way I see it, if you want the rainbow, you have to put up with the rain."

-Dolly Parton

42.
Get Up When Life Knocks You Down

As you try to pursue your dreams and goals, you will undoubtedly encounter obstacles that will knock you down. Whether you achieve your dreams and goals will largely depend on your willingness to get up when life knocks you down. You will be knocked down, because it happens to everyone. The question is, will you get up? Those who are willing to keep getting up every time they are knocked down succeed in life.

"Never surrender to adversity!"
-James Malinchak

43.
Hard Work Pays Off

The thrill of achieving a goal is knowing that you put in the time and worked hard for it. Whether it's helping a charity, receiving a promotion, landing a big account or reaching a higher income level. The satisfaction of knowing that it was your dedication, commitment and effort is what makes achieving a goal worthwhile.

"Opportunity is missed by most people because it is dressed in overalls and looks like work."

-Thomas Edison

44.
Practice Good Habits

There's an old saying, "Repetition is the mother of skill," meaning that in order to improve or increase performance, you need to continuously practice the appropriate strategies. Studies indicate that it takes approximately 21-30 days to create a new habit. This means that if you want to change or create a belief in your mind, it should become a natural habit after working on it for 21-30 days.

"We are what we repeatedly do.
Excellence, then, is not an act, but a habit."
-Aristotle

"We first make our habits and then our habits make us."
–John Dryden

45.
Get Rid of the Excuses

Too many people focus on excuses rather than solutions. Any excuse you give yourself for not pursuing what you desire will be justified. If you always focus on the excuses why you can't achieve your goals, then you'll never find the solutions for *how* you can achieve your goals. When faced with an obstacle get rid of the excuses and focus on solutions for overcoming the obstacle.

"Ninety-nine percent of failures come from people who have the habit of making excuses."

-George Washington Carver

46.
Always Believe in Yourself

As you pursue your dreams and goals you may encounter people who tell you that you're not smart enough to succeed. You may encounter people who tell you that you don't have the ability to succeed. And you will certainly encounter people who just don't believe in you or your abilities. So if you don't believe in yourself and what you are trying to accomplish, then who will?

"If I believe I cannot do something, it makes me incapable of doing it. But when I believe I can, I acquire the ability to do it, even if I did not have the ability in the beginning."

-Mahatma Gandhi

47.
Take Advantage of Opportunities

One thing we all have in common no matter what our age is opportunity. We have the opportunity to achieve success. The difference is that some of us take advantage of situations and go on to achieve success while others let situations take advantage of them. If you allow situations to take advantage of you then you are really selling yourself short of achieving your dreams and goals.

REMEMBER:

"If it's going to be, then it's up to me."
-Unknown

48.
Be Thankful for Good Health and Safety

One thing you should never do is to take life for granted. Be thankful for what you have and don't get angry or resentful about what you don't have. Many people around the world are not as fortunate as you. Remember, as long as you have good health and safety you have everything. Nothing is more important. Not money, cars, fame or job status. Without good health and safety, nothing else seems to matter.

"Many of the things you can count, don't count. Many of the things you can't count, really count."

-Albert Einstein

49.
Help Others

No matter what our status or age, one thing everyone can do is help others. One of the best feelings you can have is when you know in your heart, that you have made a difference in someone's life by helping them. Wouldn't this world be a better place if everyone had an attitude of helping others?

"Everybody can be great because anybody can serve. You don't have to have a college degree to serve. You don't have to make your subject and verb agree to serve. You only need a heart full of grace. A soul generated by love."

-Dr. Martin Luther King, Jr.

50.
Don't Just Sit There, Take Action

Whether you achieve your dreams and goals is solely up to you. No one can do it for you. No one can promise or guarantee what level of success you will achieve. However, by following simple success strategies like those in this book, YOU WILL begin to achieve the level of success you desire.

**YOU CAN DO IT –
THE TIME TO START IS NOW!**

"You miss 100% of the shots you never take."
-Wayne Gretzky
Legendary Hockey Player